DOCKLAND
BUILDINGS
OLD AND NEW

DOCKLAND BUILDINGS
OLD AND NEW

A Personal, Anecdotal
and
Historical Guide

Written and photographed by
James Page-Roberts

The Mudlark Press

British Library Cataloguing-in-publication data

A catalogue record for this book is available through the British Library

First published in 1998 by The Mudlark Press
PO Box 13729, London W6 9GN

Photographs and map © James Page-Roberts

Design and typeset by Ray Leaning, Smart Credits

Printed and bound by Biddles, Guildford, Surrey

Cover design by Robert Page-Roberts

ISBN 0 9530517 2 2

CONTENTS

I would like to thank my family, Margreet, Robert and Peter, for their help. I dedicate this book to them.

I would also like to thank Corydon Unwin for his critical and constructive eye, and Andrew Davies for his knowledgeable and helpful comments.

Books also written by the author include:
GUIDE TO A DOCKLAND OF CHANGE
(The Mudlark Press)

CANARY WHARF AND SIGHTS FROM
DOCKLANDS LIGHT RAIL
(The Mudlark Press)

VINES IN YOUR GARDEN
(Argus Books)

THE BEST WINE IN THE SUPER MARKET
(Foulsham)

The first three editions of
THE BEST WINE BUYS IN THE HIGH STREET
(Foulsham)

THE OLDIE COOKBOOK
(The Carbery Press)

VINES AND WINES IN A SMALL GARDEN
(The Herbert Press/A&C Black)

WINES FROM A SMALL GARDEN
(Abbeville Press, New York)

DRUIF EN WIJN UIT EIGEN TUIN
(Schuyt, Haarlem)

About This Book

BUILDINGS

To love buildings is to love history and to love life. For those who do, whether travelling a hundred paces or around the world, not a second will be boring and not a moment wasted.

The act of obtaining pleasure from architecture cannot be experienced too early or too late in life. Appreciation will come, simply from observation - with a little help from guides and reference books. Study in depth if you will, but in order to obtain enormous pleasure from looking at buildings or parts of them, there is no actual need. A keen eye for shapes, textures and ornamentation is all that is required.

You may favour ancient or modern, simple or grand. Even buildings from a period not particularly to your taste will grow on you in time as their style becomes more familiar or fashion changes your views.

The tastes of those who commission or create buildings are often out of line with "modern" ideas so they will opt for copies of buildings of a style that has past. Contemporary ideas become incorporated into these mock designs, giving the neo-game away. The materials used, thickness of walls and window construction are also some of the clues to this deception.

You may not be interested in many buildings of recent construction, often presented in groups, the plans for which appear to have been taken by numbers from the architect's drawer. They have been simply thrown up to make as much money as quickly as possible. Perhaps some will become monuments to the quick buck.

WHAT DOCKLAND HAS TO OFFER

Docklands are steeped in the very history of this country - especially the naval and sea trading part of it. Although nearly all of the ancient wooden buildings, wharfage and slipways have long since gone, bricks and mortar, in the form of several churches, pubs, schools, warehouses, with examples of dockland domestic architecture, remain for us to see. And there are still fascinating indications here and there of the hustle and bustle of London's glorious riverside past. With these, and a good stretch of the imagination, we can see into history.

MY CHOICE

Described without prejudice, my choice of buildings in Docklands is a very personal and unprofessional one. Some large, some small, some ancient, some new, all have intrigued me for one reason or another since first setting foot in the area some fifty or more years ago.

I offer short descriptions in plain language on my reasons for choosing as I have. Locations are on the map. But your own choice is as valid as mine. And buildings of enormous interest and significance may be revealed to you if you walk around with a keen eye. That's the fun of it all.

TAKE YOUR TIME

By wandering you will get a feel for Docklands, its atmosphere and people. To rush would be a shame. You would then miss so much. Breaks for food and drink will bring you into closer touch with the people. So do not be afraid to engage in conversation at every opportunity. Friendliness seems to be a trait of the inhabitants of this vibrant part of the world.

HOW TO USE THE BOOK

I will describe my chosen buildings in sequence and when seen when wandering on foot.

Start at the beginning of any route, or even start in the middle of one. End when you are tired. Whenever there is a chance to go home by bus or Underground I mention it and tell you how.

It is handier and probably cheaper to buy a One Day Travelcard that will allow for unlimited travel by Underground or bus from 09.30 in the morning until midnight. A 3 zone ticket will cover all routes. Monument Underground Station, which is an ideal place from which to set off on Route 1, is reached by the District Line or Circle Line. It is also connected by passageways and staircases to Bank, which is served by the Central Line, Waterloo & City Line, Northern Line and Docklands Light Rail.

I give rough distances for each route, measured by pedometer and map measurer. To gauge the time that any one will take, estimate that you might walk at about two to three miles per hour - that is, if not taking breaks for refreshment, or diversions and detours to see the sights, such as the Tower of London or Museum in Docklands. So that, too, must be a very rough estimate.

I have captioned the photographs by bold capitals in the text. Any other buildings or items of special interest are indicated in bold type, with pub names also in bold for their refreshment and conveniences.

Prepare for unexpected weather. And wrap up well in the wintertime.

Or read the book in an arm chair or in bed.

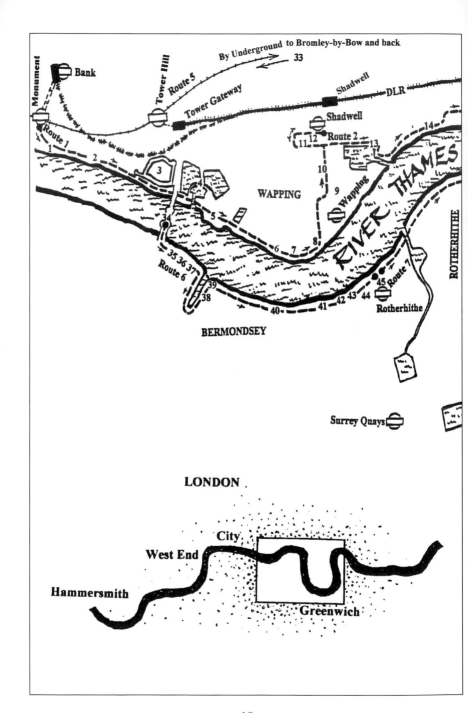

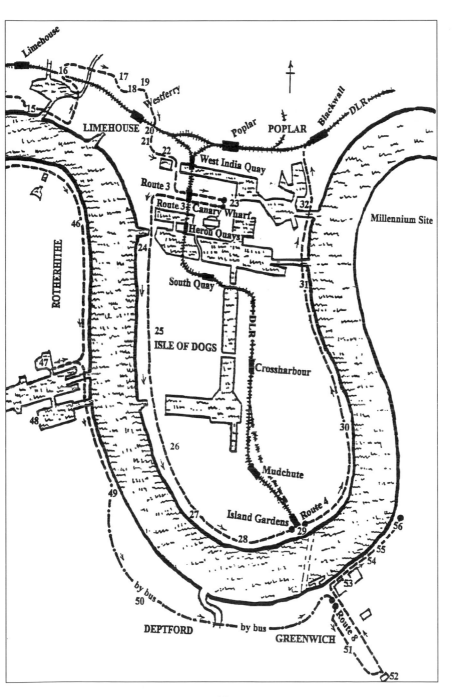

ROUTE 1

FROM OLD BILLINGSGATE FISH MARKET AND THE TOWER OF LONDON TO SHADWELL

(by foot roughly 2⅓ miles or 3.75 kilometres)

This route takes you from the City of London through an area that was once the busiest in Docklands.

Leave Monument Underground Station by the exit indicating The Monument. Turn right as you leave the station and you are beneath Sir Christopher Wren's **Monument** (1671-1677) that commemorates the Great Fire of London (1666). The height of the Monument, with its gilded flame on top of a fluted column, is the same as its distance from the bakery in Pudding Lane where the fire started. There are 311 steps should you want to climb up inside for a view over London - recommended but tiring. Note Caius Gabriel Cibber's fine bas-relief on the pedestal. This depicts the destruction created by the Great Fire of London on the left hand side. On the right, Charles II, dressed strangely in Roman costume with a semi-naked lady at hand, directs rebuilding operations. A most dissatisfied devil fumes beneath him in disgust.

Continue past the bas-relief straight down Fish Street Hill, to cross busy Lower Thames Street at the traffic lights. Turn left into Lower Thames Street, and after the overhead pedestrian bridge turn right to the river side and Thames Path. Turn left, and shortly you will reach the **OLD BILLINGSGATE FISH MARKET** (1877 and designed by Sir Horace Jones). Here is a great place to view it and the river vista.

A fine building for a fish market, it is made of London Stock bricks and stone columns, topped by golden fish weather vanes. A larger dock here was in use in the 1300s, and by 1598 it was the most important landing place in London for fish and other commodities. In time, only fishing boats moored alongside the quay to deliver their catch for sale. When efficient road and rail deliveries from other ports took over, and the market became too busy and too cramped, it moved to Poplar in 1982. In the early morning the area around the old market was totally congested with vans, fish porters with barrows, and porters with round fish baskets and wooden boxes on their heads. The noise was considerable. After the market was over, all was swept clean and hosed down. Then the normal traffic of Lower Thames Street could proceed. But the fishy smell remained. At great expense, offices have now replaced the stalls of fish for sale.

Return to Lower Thames Street up the side of the old market through Old Billingsgate Walk. Turn right to reach the large and imposing **CUSTOM HOUSE** (1817). It was from here that I used to be cleared, in the early 1950s, before walking to Limehouse to join ship at Dundee Wharf, or sometimes having to find my way further down river to Barking Creek. As a mere matelot supernumerary, I do not recall passing through the enormous and forbidding doors but, for a century (the 19th) or more, everyone who paid their dues or settled for dutiable goods did. The building's formidable facade must have been designed to impress the honest and deter the rest. The river side of the building is notable, as is the Long Room inside.

My 1950s walks to Limehouse were not the first introductions to Docklands, the East End, its buildings and people. While stationed at RAF Hornchurch waiting to learn to fly in the USA during the war, I volunteered to become a slater to mend bombed-out roofs in Plumstead. Depressing as it was in its bombed and poverty-stricken state, I learned that here was a magical part of London - especially the busy riverside with its huge and imposing warehouse buildings. It was on a Plumstead roof that I witnessed a great explosion not far away, followed by a very strange swoosh, like a gale of wind. It was one of the first German V2 rockets to strike London.

Do not bear left up hill, but continue along the Lower Thames Street pavement after passing Custom House and you will see the Tower of London in front of you. Just before you reach it, almost immediately on the left at the bottom of Tower Hill, there is a little round tower (1869) standing on its own. This is a fascinating item of London's history. Twenty-six years after the financially unsuccessful first under-Thames tunnel was built by Brunel, another was commissioned for pedestrians near to the Tower (Tower Bridge had not yet been built). A 26 year old South African born engineer, called Greathead, took on the job, designing his own tunnelling machine. He completed the tunnel to Vine Lane on the other side of the river within a year, and in 1870 the Tower Subway was opened for an under river cable car service. As this system did not produce an adequate income, it became a walkway with an annual passage of over a million people. And the tunnel was only 6'7" (2 metres approx.) in diameter with a spiral staircase at either end! When Tower Bridge was opened in 1894 the tunnel became redundant, and is now closed to the public and used for water mains and cables. The lettering around the tower is a passing claim of ownership by the London Hydraulic Company, who used it for their high pressure pipes at one time.

3

Almost certainly of Roman origin, the **Tower of London** was sited to command a prime position on rising ground with marshes and the river for added protection. This massive fortress covers a moated, hexagonal area of irregular shape,

3

enclosing a splendid Norman Keep, known as the White
Tower. This 1078 inner fortification contains one of the finest
and simplest places of religion in England, the **NORMAN
CHAPEL OF ST. JOHN**. For that alone it is worth a visit to
the Tower. Of course there is a lot more to see there, the
Crown Jewels being among them.

The Tower has served in many roles, as bastion, palace, prison, place of execution and burial. From the outside it is as forbidding as fortresses must be. Its Traitors' Gate adds to this feeling of apprehension. Through it, by boat from the river, passed many a soul for the first and last time.

Names connected with the Tower are many, both famous and infamous - Henry VI, the young Princes in the Tower, Queen Elizabeth I, Sir Thomas More (who, after execution, had his head spiked upon London Bridge), Anne Boleyn, Katharine Howard (both Henry VIII's wives), Lady Jane Grey, Dudley, the Duke of Monmouth... Now the Beef-eaters, Yeoman Warders, guard and guide without malice.

The beautifully weathered stonework of the castle walls gives the whole a feeling of strength, history, age and power. Without even buying a ticket it is easy to appreciate its ancient construction by glancing at the stones of the 1280 **BYWARD TOWER** (the first tower beyond the moat by the entrance to the castle).

From the river bank you may see modern **mudlarks** with metal-detectors and spades digging around in the mud of the foreshore at low tide. They are looking for historical artefacts - swords, bronze torsos, crowns and things (tunnellers of the Tower Subway found a bag of 300 Henry III silver coins here). The child mudlarks of the 18th and 19th century, and there were many of them in this vicinity, also prowled around, but to scrape some kind of a living from the river. The word "mudlark" can mean an extraordinary number of things, but The New English Dictionary on Historical Principles of the late 19th century has this delightful definition: "... so called from their being accustomed to prowl about at low water under the quarter of West India ships under pretence of grubbing in the mud for old ropes, iron, etc., but whose chief object was to receive and conceal small bags of sugar, coffee, etc. which they conveyed to such thieves as they were directed, and for which services they generally received a share of the booty."

4

Keep close to the River Thames and glance in front and to the right of you for a sight of **Tower Bridge** (we will come to it later at the start of Route 6) and, passing through an archway beneath Tower Bridge (where a real cannon from the Napoleonic wars acts as a bollard), you will come to the bridged entrance and **St. Katharine Dock**. Here, set proudly in the middle, is the **IVORY HOUSE**. A building like it existed there at the time of the dock's construction in 1828, but the one you see now was designed by George Aitcheson in 1854. The Dockmaster's House at the river entrance is original. The Ivory House was a warehouse handling scents and shells from the Orient, as well as ivory.

You may want to wander around here, possibly to look at the yachts and motor vessels, to eat at the several cafés, drink beer or wine, or dine at the **Dickens Inn**. The inn's wooden facade and some interior woodwork formed part of the construction of a brewery warehouse on the river nearby. It was dismantled and cleverly incorporated into the modern pub.

5

Keeping as near to the river as possible in St. Katharine's Way, a white building stands out most boldly at number 84 (on the right, and river side). It is the **SUMMIT** building of offices. Best seen at low tide from the river shore, it contrasts splendidly with the ancient wooden piles at the waterside in front of it. Reach the shore by taking Alderman Stairs at low tide. These "stairs" (and there are several more along both river banks) were taken by watermen and their passengers when the river was teeming with sailing ships.

Across the river you will see the large **Butler's Wharf** and the white **Design Museum**. We will come to them on Route 6.

6

Continue along St. Katharine's Way, passing Hermitage
Basin on the left (an old entrance to London Dock and a
much earlier tidal mill pool). Now the road becomes Wapping
High Street where, before the bombing of London by the
Germans and post war demolition, you could not see the river
for enormous warehouses on their riverside wharves. After
where modern buildings have sprung up at the bend in the
road, you will suddenly come to the terraced **PIERHEAD**
houses, built on either side of another one-time entrance to
London Dock. Notice where the lock gates were, the sides of
which have been retained. The houses were built between
1810 and 1813 for senior officials of London Dock.

The buildings, it is true, are fine, but some details are worth even more attention. See how the square section lead drainpipes are set into the walls to become decorative vertical lines on the London Stock brick surface. Note the boot-scrapers, essential at the time when roads were often unpaved and mud and horse dung abounded. And look at the extreme elegance and practical lack of ornamentation of the iron hand rails fanning out from the porches. At the street side are handsome light holders, first used for braziers, then gas lamps and finally electrical bulbs, before ending up as simple ornaments.

7

Carry on along Wapping High Street, past the **Town of Ramsgate** pub, where some think the infamous Judge Jeffreys was apprehended, and pass **Oliver' s Wharf** (one of the early conversions from Victorian warehouse to living accommodation) and take a left hand turning at Pierhead Wharf, along Scandrett Street. On the right hand side you will see **ST. JOHN OF WAPPING SCHOOL**. The school was founded in 1695 and the boy and girl in their separate niches are dressed as they would have been then. To me, these old schools, with pupils strictly segregated, exude an air of discipline and unhappiness. But today they are splendidly decorative (we come to another in Rotherhithe on Route 6).

Return to Wapping High Street, noting the walkways, catwalks or flying bridges above that were once such a feature of Docklands. Pass the mould-fronted Metropolitan Police Boat Yard, a little park and the Police Station (where there are excellent steps from which to view the river). Continue on your way, past the **Captain Kidd** pub, until you see King Henry's Stairs on the right (the sign is high up on the wall) and Brewhouse Lane on the left. On your right, as you look down the alleyway to the stairs, stood Execution Dock. Here, malefactors were hanged, tied to the river bed and covered by three tides. They were then wired, tarred for preservation and dangled from gibbets on Millwall (and at the Millennium site in Greenwich) to deter sailors approaching London with villainous intent. Turn to the left (around a cannon bollard) into Brewhouse Lane.

From here you can see a building up to the left in Brewhouse Lane that intrigued me for years. Could it be new? Could it be old? Were they flats, modern or old? And when were flats, as such, first conceived and built? I stopped to look and then passed by, always thinking that the building's proportions were splendid, and left it at that.

Then one day I walked up Brewhouse Lane to investigate. At the rear I found most elegant cast iron balustrades and tiny staircases. And at the corner of the block, all was revealed in bold lettering: **TOWER BUILDINGS**, ERECTED BY THE IMPROVED INDUSTRIAL DWELLINGS COMPANY (LIMITED) 1864.

I learned from an inhabitant that the flats are very small and that each should have been joined to another at a time of restoration. And the windows, that to me looked so grand and balanced in the design, let in so much sunlight that to live there is at times like being in a sauna. But Tower Buildings is still among my favourite in Docklands.

9

Tower Buildings are on a corner of Brewhouse Lane. Turn right there, and then left into the community of Wapping Lane - the only "village" with shops and pubs in Wapping.

You will have already seen, and see now, many, many 1930s blocks of Council accommodation. Most have been upgraded, with the original windows replaced by ones made of a more practical material. But the buildings are bare of decoration, which they so desperately need. Some residents make the very best of their balconies and public passageways by growing flowers, sometimes tomatoes and very occasionally a grape vine. This helps to break up the endless expanses of yellow brick. But there, having turned to the left into Wapping Lane, look right, down **PRUSOM STREET**, and you will see one of these blocks with its end almost covered with ivy and creeper - improving the looks of the locality no end.

Of the other two instances that I have noticed where decoration has been allowed to break up the monotony of blocks, one is at the corner of Deptford Church Street and Frankham Street, in Deptford, where a plaster surface has been painted as a relief on the Lewisham Housing

CROSSFIELD ESTATE, Crossfield Tenants' Collective, and the other on **ARAGON TOWER** by the River Walk, south of South Greenland Dock. Here, white masks adorn dark brickwork. Both of these places appear on Route 7.

9

9

From Brewhouse Lane you have turned left into Wapping Lane. Continue past the **White Swan and Cuckoo, Three Swedish Crowns** and **Turner's Old Star** pubs. Then on your right you will come to **St. Peter, London Docks**, a church that looks rather like a monastery from the street. It was designed by J.F. Pownall in 1866. Enter to experience a view of unaltered high Victorian splendour. Next you walk up hill to where there was once a swing bridge where cargo ships, tugs and barges crossed from Eastern Dock of London Dock on the right, through to Tobacco Dock and then on to Western Dock on the left. The **TOBACCO DOCK** entrance is to the left just across the "bridge". Enter and make your way to the lower floor where from between 1811 to 1814 a magnificent vaulted brick ceiling was constructed, supported by very primitive stone and granite pillars (almost African). The warehouse (very much larger than the one you see now) was made to hold tobacco, but the enormous vaults were more used for the storage of wine and spirits. After tobacco, the ground floor was mainly used for fleeces. Because of this, the dock was often known as the "Skin Floor".

Interesting, four branched, cast iron supports were cleverly designed to support the warehouse's timber, glass and slate roof. And rainwater was ducted below to keep the wooden pilings moist. There is much here to interest the architect.

11

Continue up Wapping Lane, or exit from the other end of Tobacco Dock (where just inside there is a café and also public conveniences) and a bit to the left in front of you, across the Highway, stands Nicholas Hawksmoor's **ST. GEORGE-IN-THE-EAST.**

Queen Anne asked Parliament for money in 1711 to build churches to commemorate Marlborough's victories on the continent. With also the heretical tendencies of London's growing population in mind, they granted it (the 50 New Churches Act of 1711), taxing coal entering London by water to finance the project. Of the many proposed only a few were built. St. George-in-the-East was one. Another, St. Anne's, we come to soon on Route 2.

St. George-in-the-East was completed in 1724 and remained intact until the Blitz in 1941, when fire destroyed the roof and interior. The inside was very cleverly refashioned in 1964 with an inner courtyard, reducing the size of the church and creating living accommodation.

When I stand and raise my eyes close to its west end I feel as though I am looking up the face of a stone quarry.

12

Exit from the front of the church and turn right into Cannon Street Road. Then turn right into Cable Street to be completely surprised to see on the right hand side an intact terrace of beautiful **GEORGIAN HOUSES** - and all this in an area of characterless Council blocks. Perhaps that is why the terrace seems even more impressive. One house is larger than the others. It is thought that the owner or builder lived there. In the middle is a shop - a real Georgian one. The fact that there is often rubbish lying outside the houses, presumably attracting vermin, actually adds to the 18th centuriness of it all.

When I first stood to admire this terrace, I fully expected that a voice might say: "Cut. Thank you. You can all go home". And out of the doors would come actors and actresses in 18th century costume as stage hands would strike the set and pack the painted flats away for yet another period "soap".

We have come to the end of Route 1 and the start of Route 2.

Beyond the 18th century terrace in Cable Street is Shadwell Underground Station. From here you could return to Central London, changing at Whitechapel. Or you might cross the river to Rotherhithe (end of Route 6 and start of route 7). Or you could walk just a little further on and turn left into Watney Street to pass Peter's Pie and Mash shop (eels on Fridays), the **Old House at Home** pub and enter the Shadwell DLR Station to either return to Tower Gateway or Bank, or go on to Island Gardens via Canary Wharf. So should you have become tired, there are plenty of escape routes here.

ROUTE 2

FROM SHADWELL TO CANARY WHARF
(by foot roughly 3 miles or 4.75 kilometres)

This route takes you from the defunct London Dock, through the Chinatown of old to West India Dock and the modern development of Canary Wharf.

13

Should you be starting with Route 2, alight at Shadwell DLR Station, turn left into Watney Street and right into Cable Street for the Georgian terrace and onward. Or reach Shadwell Station on the East London Line and turn right into Cable Street as you leave the station. Or, if continuing from Route 1, retrace your steps along the Georgian terrace in Cable Street and turn left back into Cannon Street Road. Turn left around **St. George-in-the-East** and cross the busy Highway.

On the right you will soon come to the church of **ST. PAUL'S, SHADWELL**, the crypt of which dates from around 1656 and the building above it 1820. Its tower is one of the most elegant, if not *the* most elegant, in Docklands.

If St. George-in-the-East commemorated Marlborough's victories, St. Paul's was erected to thank heaven for Wellington's success over Napoleon. But its leanings have always been toward the sea, not the land, as many sea captains are buried there. **Captain Cook** worshipped in the church and his son was baptised there. President **Thomas Jefferson**'s mother, **Jane Randolph**, was also baptised in the church. She then clearly sailed to America as Thomas Jefferson was born in Shadwell, Albemarle County, Virginia.

Turn right (down hill) into Glamis Road, where you can see the Canary Wharf tower on the left, and walk toward the bascule bridge that was once raised to allow shipping in and out of the extensive London Dock. Look into Shadwell Basin on the right. Down the road in front of you, by the riverside, is the **Prospect of Whitby**, a famous dockland pub. To the right, beyond the bridge, stands the red brick **London Hydraulic Power Company**'s ivy-clad accumulator tower and Pumping Station. Built in 1890, with a gate house of 1891, this power station and accumulator, with four others, supplied all who needed hydraulic power in central London. Through 184 miles of pressure mains (400 lbs per square inch) it worked equipment in many docks, iron safety curtains in theatres, the two bascules of Tower Bridge (until 1974), and lifts in buildings through much of the capital. The Company closed down in 1977. Now many of the pipes house optical fibre cables.

Just before you reach the bascule bridge, turn left along a narrow alleyway. You will come to a pleasant park on the left (**King Edward VII Gardens**, or Park) situated where once a thoroughly insalubrious part of London stood, with fish market, brothels and drinking dens. The district was popular with sailors.

The circular brick ventilation shaft in front of you extracts noxious air from the **Rotherhithe Road Tunnel** that crosses beneath the Thames at this point (you will see its other ventilation shaft across the river). Beside the shaft is a tablet to commemorate the Armada hero and explorer, Sir Martin

Frobisher and naval heroes Steven and William Borough and Sir Hugh Willoughby. They all sailed from near to this spot.

The view over the water is one of the best. It is a good place for a rest should you feel like one. There are several well positioned benches on the bank side, where once dockers and retired people took their rest in the sunshine. Continue.

14

When the strange, red brick building of **FREE TRADE WHARF** flats (in front of you and at the water side) was constructed in the late 1980s, I disliked it intensely, though I am sure it is an excellent place in which to live, with views of the river for the residents so cleverly contrived by the architects. Then one day I was there when bright sunlight struck one facet and then another, creating quickly changing areas of light and shade. Perhaps I am coming around to quite liking it.

15

Continue along the River Walk until you reach the two handsome **warehouses** (1870) **of Free Trade Wharf**. Walk between them and through the 1796 three arched gateway to turn right into the Highway. You will breathe in too many fumes from traffic on this busy stretch. Pass Atlantic Wharf. As you reach the traffic lights where the Limehouse Link and Rotherhithe road tunnels surface, and Butcher Row leads off to the left, look along Butcher Row to see on the right hand side of it a very fine house, built in 1796 for one Matthew Whiting. It is now the **Royal Foundation of St. Katharine**, an ancient religious foundation founded by Queen Matilda in 1147 as the Hospital of St. Katharine by the Tower (Tower of London). The buildings were demolished in 1825 to make room for St. Katharine Dock. After WW2 the Foundation was re-established here in Butcher Row. Held tightly between two busy road tunnels and Limehouse DLR Station, the house and gardens form a peaceful retreat and conference centre.

A short walk up Butcher Row and first right into Ratcliffe Walk will lead you to Limehouse DLR Station. So here is another "go home" point should you feel tired.

From where you saw the two tunnels and Butcher Row, turn right into Narrow Street just beyond the lights. In front of you at the bend in the road are Ratcliff Cross Stairs and Causeway. If the tide is low take the stairs (be careful as they, like most stairs, are often slippery) and walk along the river shore until you reach a water outflow. In front and on the left you will see part of one of the finest conversions on the river, built by Sir David Lean, the film director, at **SUN WHARF**, 30 Narrow Street. Demolished warehouses have made room for a delightful small garden, and the house, still privately owned, contains all that such a man could desire. It has been designed with simplicity and, surprisingly, very little theatricality. Most of the internal walls are of unplastered, London Stock brick. The house is not open to the public.

Return to walk down Narrow Street, turning right down an alleyway next to the aforementioned house after you have passed a warehouse with a tree apparently growing out of the top of it. Continue, taking the road or River Walk, past the entrance to **Limehouse Basin,** and after that the **Grapes** pub (which Charles Dickens is thought to have frequented, though others believe that it was a pub a few doors down at 98).

16

The Grapes is attached to a fine **terrace of 18th century houses**, spoiled on the river side. Another pub, the **House They Left Behind**, is over to the left, and yet another, **Booty's** to the right. You then come to a park on the left with gates made of tubular steel. Go through them, cross **The Cut** (a very early canal, 1770, the other end of which you will see at Bow Locks on Route 5) and you will notice on the left beyond an arch, a small, octagonal, brick building with a chimney stack to match. This building is the **REGENT'S CANAL DOCK BOILER CHIMNEY AND ACCUMULATOR TOWER**, built in 1869.

The boiler has gone. The tower and chimney were important as they provided hydraulic pressure to operate the lock gates, capstans, cranes and swing bridge connected with the dock (now Limehouse Basin and Marina). The tower contains a weight-loaded hydraulic accumulator that ensured even pressure to all the machinery, regardless of how much was demanded at any one time. Because of its charm and simplicity it is one of my favourite buildings in Docklands. It is also visible from the DLR, but being so near to the rails, comes and goes in a flash.

Retrace your steps a little and pass through another DLR arch, around a small bronze foundry (the Limehouse Gallery), to reach busy Commercial Road. Turn right into it and then shortly right again into **Newell Street**. In this part 18th century thoroughfare you will see on the left **ST. ANNE'S, LIMEHOUSE**, towering into the sky. This Nicholas Hawksmoor (1724, finished 1730) church is, like St. George-in-the-East, another Queen Anne, coal tax funded church, clearly constructed to impress East Enders. And impressive it is in the power and weight of its design. The tower was once a major landmark for shipping on the river, and the clock (added later), thought to be the highest church clock in England, must have been invaluable to those from a watchless age.

17

Note a **pyramidal memorial** on the left as you enter the churchyard. Hawksmoor wanted two of them to decorate the eastern end of the church but only one was supplied. He dumped it in the churchyard. So it has almost become a memorial to him. Exit on the far side into Three Colt Street by the **Five Bells and Bladebone** pub.

18

The practically built Victorian pub and the small scale but very grand moulded-brick terracotta Victorian Institute beside it, form a splendid pair of contrasting 19th century buildings. In days before radio and television the **LIMEHOUSE CHURCH INSTITUTE** was designed to supply the spiritual needs of the locals and the **FIVE BELLS AND BLADEBONE** the desires of thirst and entertainment. A brothel next door would have completed the Victorian picture. Perhaps there was one.

19

Return to busy Commercial Road to the left up Three Colt Street, which was once the main artery to and from the Isle of Dogs, and then turn right. At the bend, and on the other side of the busy thoroughfare, you will see the small **VICTORIAN FUNERAL PARLOUR** of Francis & C. Walters Ltd. This fine reminder of an East End of the past may have even earlier origins. Admire it from outside. Inside it is partitioned off with fibreboard from a later age. Note the Victorian edifice of the **Star of the East** pub two doors away.

Bear right into West India Dock Road, which, with Limehouse Causeway and Pennyfields was once the heart of **Chinatown**, with eating places, Charlie Brown's pub, gambling dens and all the rest that made it a colourful setting for sordid tales by authors from Charles Dickens onwards. Cleaned up, opened up and sanitised, a few restaurants and the **Oporto** pub remain. The modern Chinatown has moved to the West End of London, centred on Gerrard Street and its environs.

20

Cross the intersection where Westferry Road ducts away traffic to Canary Wharf and the Isle of Dogs, and pass through the first archway of the DLR on the right. This will lead you into Garford Street. In it and on the left are 1819 **houses for dock police** (the Sergeant got the largest, naturally). Before you reach them you will see the gate to **GREIG HOUSE** (1911). This most decorative and beautifully coloured stock and moulded red brick building, built in the William and Mary style with copper clad clock tower and cupola, belonged to Sweden in the heyday of West India Dock. It was used by the officers of the Swedish merchant shipping fleet and as a Mission. In the 1930s the building was given to the Salvation Army, who also own the monstrous 1902 Hostel block next to it.

21

Return to where you entered Garford Street and turn right, past the rear of Greig House (seen now with difficulty), past the handsome **Dockmaster's House** (1807, and once a rough and tumble inn and never used by a Dockmaster) and on through No.1 Gate into West India Dock. Pass the Dock Company's Police building (1914), again on the right, to see a small, round, brick building at the entrance to Cannon Workshops. There were once two of them, one an **ARMOURY** and the other a temporary **LOCK-UP** for dock thieves. The one existing building was probably the armoury. I find it to be a gem of a construction among so many massive neighbours.

22

A nd it is to one of those massive buildings that we come to next on the left at **WEST INDIA QUAY**. Cleaned of their wall-mounted cranes and other working paraphernalia, these massive **early 19th century sugar, molasses, rum and coffee warehouses**, stretched even further along the dock. But the far end was bombed and destroyed in the war. Their size and position epitomise the importance of shipping and docks in 19th century London. It is absolutely appropriate that Warehouse No.1 (the nearest to you) should house the **Museum in Docklands**, telling the history and life of London's port and river.

23

Take the foot bridge that you see before you across the dock, and climb steps to Cabot Square with its fountain and waterfalls. You are now in the **Canary Wharf** complex (called so because thin-skinned bananas were once brought here from the Canary Islands).

Look at Cesar Pelli's tower, **ONE CANADA SQUARE**. It

is 50 floors of steel and concrete, clad in glass and stainless steel. Containing offices, and not open to the public, it can sway 13¾" (35 cm) in the highest wind, reflect the passing of clouds, and sparkle in the sunshine. Cosy (if one can call any such a large object so) at close quarters and not seemingly especially tall, it stands out as a splendid landmark from not only all over Docklands but from most of London, too.

Mr. Pelli's tower is one of my three favourites (the other two being the Chrysler in New York and the Bank of China in Hong Kong) because of its uncannily clever proportions. And being surrounded by less imaginative buildings give it even greater significance.

Steps down on either side of Cabot Square lead you to either **Fisherman's Walk** or **Mackenzie Walk**. Here there are excellent pubs and restaurants where you may eat and drink. Tables outside catch the sunshine in Mackenzie Walk and the shade in Fisherman's Walk.

Turn left in Cabot Square by the fountain and enter the Canary Wharf buildings at Cabot Place West. You are on the ground floor, one of shops, cafés and an **Information Centre**. Soon you will come to escalators up and down. Up leads you to Tesco supermarket and above that, **Gallery West**. Down takes you to the Concourse of banks, cash machines, shops and a **Post Office**. On, through doors by the Information Centre where they sell books and guides, you will see a compass rose set in the floor. Above you is the **Canary Wharf DLR Station**. So here is another chance to go home if you have had enough walking. Or you might want to skip the Routes around the Isle of Dogs and take the DLR onwards to Island Gardens and Greenwich (Route 8).

Go through yet another set of heavy doors to Cabot Place East where above and below are shops, restaurants and the **Books etc**. book shop. Below is the public convenience. And that is where we end Route 2.

ROUTE 3

THE WESTERN SIDE
OF THE ISLE OF DOGS
(by foot roughly 3 miles or 4.75 kilometres)

*This route takes you around half of the Isle of Dogs,
an area originally of marsh land, windmills, and
bodies suspended from gibbets. Then, from the
Industrial Revolution, it was a place of wharves,
ship building, industry, coal smoke, and
extreme dirt, grime and poverty.
For routes 3 & 4 there will be more walking and less
of interest to see. But there will still be plenty to attract
and surprise you. It is worth remembering that the
roads, warehouses and industry that surrounded the
Isle of Dogs when the port was in full swing were
among the roughest of places imaginable.
And amazingly, in the post war years, many
of its pubs were known for their drag shows,
which always struck me as being
most incongruous.*

24

If starting anew on Route 3, get to Canary Wharf DLR Station. Otherwise retrace your steps past Canary Wharf shops, cafés, etc., walk past the fountain of Cabot Square and take the left hand side of the dual carriageway of West India Avenue to the busy Westferry Circus. Make for the centre of it if you want to take a "framed" photograph of Cesar Pelli's tower (One Canada Square).

Turn left at the lights in the Circus, and take the very narrow pavement on the right hand side of the road leading down to Westferry Road. As you go down you will see in front and on the riverside to the right, **CASCADES** (1987), a tall building of flats, full of ideas and nautical motifs, situated where once stood a confectionery factory. Best seen from a boat on the river, it is a building (when seen from the side, looking not unlike a ski slope) that continues to please by its audacity. If only more buildings in Dockland exhibited as much imagination and fun as this one it would be an even more vital place.

Now cross over another busy road on your right. Continue, and beyond the cobblestone roundabout you will see the old **dock entrance** on the right and the **Pumping Station** to the left. The machinery in this red brick building tops up the West India Docks with water when necessary. Take the Thames Path down the left hand side of the dock entrance to walk between Cascades and the river. Sadly, Cascades is not quite so impressive close to. Continue, where once there were dry docks, turning left to regain Westferry Road at Anchorage Point.

It was around here that the river wall was breached in the 17th century, creating a large lake, teeming with fish, in the marshy Isle of Dogs. In the 18th century, grazing pasture on the Isle of Dogs was considered to be the best. The lake disappeared when the West India Dock was built.

Turn right into Westferry Road and walk along a bleak stretch until you see a small riverside park, **John McDougall Gardens**, on the right and the tall Bowsprit Point on the left. Turn left into the pedestrians' approach to unmarked **MELLISH STREET**.

Often, because of their gardens, there are quite a few newly built areas of domestic housing on the Isle of Dogs that give feelings of community and friendliness. Here I have picked a row of houses, set back a little on the right hand side after a short distance. This 1995 terrace of simple, utilitarian design seems to me to have got it right in proportion and decoration. And residents to whom I have spoken agree.

Return to turn left into Westferry Road, but if you peer back down Mellish Street you will get a glimpse of the **London Arena**, a dull, slab-sided building for entertainments. You would reach it and **Crossharbour DLR Station** (as possibly another "return home" point), via a terrace of

Victorian houses in Mellish Street, a kink right and left, then Pepper Street, and **Glengall Village** with the Dutch **Glengall Bridge** over **Millwall Dock**.

Now look to the right as you continue your walk down Westferry Road to see **Arnhem Wharf Primary School**, at No.114. It is modern, clean, bright, and surrounds its playground, giving a welcoming atmosphere for parents and children - a far cry from the Dickensian Isle of Dogs' schools of old.

Continue on Route 3 along Westferry Road and, having passed West Ferry Printers Limited, look in at an entrance to the **Millwall Outer Dock** on the left with its **Docklands Sailing Centre**. The dock and its vast expanse of water cry out for colour and activity. The newspaper printing works on the north quay offer some interest, but before the dock was closed to commercial traffic, beautiful Swedish Line ships tied up to the wharf where the works now stand. Having a certain notoriety, lightermen would pass close by on their barges with an eye to the portholes and the pretty stewardesses within, and were seldom disappointed.

Should you be unable to imagine the hive of industry that took place on the Isle of Dogs at the turn of the century, along quite a short stretch here on the right hand side of the road, between Nos. 154 and 308, were ships chandlers, a timber merchant, builders' merchant, beer retailer, timber preservers, cask makers, preserved provision merchant, laundry engineers, ship builders, iron works, a sailmaker, barge builders, a blacksmith, wire rope manufacturers, a sack maker, oil manufacturers, a corn dealer, warfingers, paint manufacturers, a varnish manufacturer, a colour maker, a tube maker, a coconut oil maker, a colour maker, engineers, lead manufacturers, a bronze and brass foundry, lead smelters and a white lead manufacturer. Imagine the noise, the smell and the dirt of all this industry. It could not have been a very pleasant or healthy place in which to live and work. There were many fatalities from lead poisoning.

26

A nd what is this on the left hand side at 269 Westferry Road? Is it Byzantium builded here among the dark satanic mills of the Isle of Dogs? Is it a villa from the past, perhaps? No. It is **ST. PAUL'S**, a Victorian, Presbyterian church.

Looking completely out of place now, it must have been even more so in the mid 19th century when the periphery of the Isle of Dogs was indeed made up of coal-smoked satanic slums, wharves, factories and lead mills.

John Scott Russell, builder of the mighty Great Eastern ship (we come to its launch site later, ¼ of a mile, or 360 metres, down the road), paid £750, in 1859, for this toy copy of Pisa Cathedral to house a Presbyterian Mission. John Scott Russell and architect Thomas Edward Knightly decided that the Romanesque design of this small church be made from bricks of many colours. But they were unaware that beneath the foundations lay a thick layer of unstable peat. So their charming building, containing laminated wood roof trusses (used almost for the first time), was to suffer settlement thereafter. But with most of its contemporary buildings gone, St. Paul's remains to surprise us with its jewel-like charm.

With Presbyterians moving elsewhere, the St. Paul's Arts Trust was set up in 1989 to restore the run-down building and establish a venue for the arts. With money from many worthy organisations, and much voluntary help, **The Space**, as it is now called, with its licensed café attached, consists of a centre for entertainment. Long may the building last.

27

Continue along Westferry Road and turn right at Napier Avenue to the riverside. On the left you will see the remains of a slipway where boats were built and then launched into the river (stern first). It is thought that the Great Eastern was launched here. But the **Great Eastern** was launched broadside on because the river was too narrow at this point to take so large a vessel. What remains of her real slipway may be seen at low tide on the shore.

Turn left at the river side and you come to **BURRELL'S WHARF** (1836), a Victorian wharf, with its warehouses and ironworks.

Here, **Isambard Kingdom Brunel** as designer, and **John Scott Russell** as builder, conceived and made by far the largest ship on any waters at the time (1851). It was also one of the greatest failures. To be launched sideways, this giant was designed for trade in the east, and to work under all conditions in that part of the world (even where coal was not available for her boilers). She had a double bottom, six masts and sails, enormous paddle wheels and a four-bladed screw. 692' (211 metres) in length and with 30' (9 metres) draught, she was not only the largest and most imaginative, but the strongest ship built. And yet she was a failure, mainly because Brunel hedged his bets by providing too many means of propulsion.

The first set-back came at the launch (1858), when the ship moved, and then stuck fast on the slipway for three months, causing the makers to go bankrupt. She was then purchased for the North Atlantic trade, for which she was not designed. General cargo tramp steamers took over from ships made for specific trades and she became of little worth to anyone - except that she finally redeemed herself by completing the magnificent task of laying the first Atlantic cable. In 1888 she was broken up.

Burrell's Wharf has been well converted into living accommodation. The original boiler house chimney with its iron straps still stands and is used, while the Italianate **Central Plate House**, where steel plates for the Great Eastern were produced, has been well incorporated into the whole spacious complex.

When I lived in Limehouse, some of these buildings were used as a dye works, and were famous locally for the multicoloured pigeons that flew from them.

Pass the chimney and regain Westferry Road. Turn right, and soon on the right hand side you will see **Maconochie's Wharf**, where once there was a preserved food factory and now terraces of 1989 houses, set well apart.

Continue along the road, where lead mills stood on the

right hand side, and pass **Locksfield Place** on the left. This small housing complex has some grand architectural items incorporated into the design, giving it style.

28

Now you will come to the **MILLWALL FIRE BRIGADE STATION** (1904) on the left at the junction of Westferry Road and East Ferry Road. Originally it housed only one fire engine. The horses used to pull it were kept in stables on the East Ferry Road side, behind the circular windows. To cover all of Millwall from here at a full gallop must have taxed those horses considerably.

Perhaps take the road opposite to visit the early 19th century pub, with 18th century origins, in Ferry Street, called the **Ferry House**. Displaying proudly that the hostelry is "the oldest pub on the Island", it was here that people could drink while watching out for the old Greenwich ferry to arrive.

Return to what was Westferry Road and has now become Manchester Road and turn right. Walk until you come to the

DLR bridge over the road (there are **public conveniences** on the left in front of it), and turn right there to go beneath the station to **Island Gardens**, a small park by the riverside that Sir Christopher Wren thought provided the "best view in Europe".

Here is another place from which to return home should you feel like it. Either take the DLR back to Bank or Tower Gateway via Canary Wharf, or enter the rotunda, take the lift down and the Greenwich Foot Tunnel (the pipe), and walk to the other side of the river to start on Route 8. Or, having crossed to the other side of the river, return to the Tower of London, Charing Cross or Westminster by river boat (remembering that your One Day Travelcard will not cover this water journey).

Or continue your walk around the other side of the Isle of Dogs on Route 4.

ROUTE 4

THE EASTERN SIDE
OF THE ISLE OF DOGS
(by foot roughly 2 miles or 3.5 kilometres)

*This route takes you northwards up the east
of the Isle of Dogs. This side was never as busy as
the western side. There were wharves, factories,
oil depots, shipbuilding yards and iron works,
but there was not as much dirty industry
- even though there was a manure factory
by the water.*

If deciding to make your start on Route 4, take the DLR train to Island Gardens to reach the starting point. Otherwise continue around the Isle of Dogs, keeping to the Thames Path whenever possible.

It is from here, in **ISLAND GARDENS** (created in 1895), that Sir Christopher Wren's **Royal Naval College**, the **Queen's House**, and the **Old Royal Observatory** and **Timeball** (all part of Route 8) may be seen across the river to their best advantage. It is also a good place in which to sit and rest should you need to. At 1300 hours the Timeball will fall. Then you can set your watch by genuine Greenwich time, just as navigators on the river have done since 1833.

Parallel to the river, and directly behind Islands Gardens, take Saunders Ness Road with George Green's School to your left and Luralda Gardens and more imaginative Cumberland Mills on your right, and pass the **Watermans Arms** pub on your left and the **Newcastle or Christ Church Public Draw Dock** on your right. Take the Riverside Walkway on the left, beside the dock. Look over the river toward Greenwich.

Pass Caledonian Wharf (unmarked on the river side) by Saunders Ness (the name of the river bank, recorded as such in the 16th century). In the 1840s there was shipbuilding here. You will have to go inland back to Saunders Ness Road at Storer's Quay and then regain the Riverside Walkway at Plymouth Wharf. Continue.

Now look to the left (away from the river) by the twin obelisks to see a well-proportioned square of houses called **SEXTANT AVENUE**. Off it, on the riverside, is **MARINER'S MEWS**, decorated with Dutch Gables. The modern houses in the Avenue would not look out of place in any period part of London, so cleverly have they been designed. It is housing on an imaginative and human scale.

The spicy smells of the district disappeared with the demise of the pickle factory that stood hereabouts.

Go through Sextant Avenue, passing over Saunders Ness Road, and take a narrow passageway to reach busy Manchester Road. Turn right into it, pass the **Pier Tavern** (where the cellar ghost, called Ginger, likes turning on taps and is a confounded nuisance) and in a while look over to the left to see the brick, white paint and stucco **Jubilee Crescent**. This mid 1930s housing for retired ship workers, with its balconies supported by square-section pillars, is unlike any other on the Isle of Dogs, and is a welcome sight after passing so many large blocks of flats. The garden in front was once a bowling green.

To the right, behind Millennium Court and Millennium Wharf, was Millwall Wharf. Here I gave the Captain of the Spanish coaster MV Indunaval Primero about £30 in 1966 to bring me back some table wine from Valencia. He returned with two elongated casks strapped to the railings on deck. I paid duty and, with difficulty, transported them home. Second hand bottles were far too expensive at 6d each, but the dealer in them told me that he collected empties from the large hotels. So I took mine from outside restaurants before the rubbish men got there in the early hours of the morning. After two nights collecting I had acquired around 300 claret bottles - for free. And then, after giving them a wash, bottled 94 litres of 16 grados and 90 litres of 15 grados red wine. I had started to import wine for home consumption. So I have happy memories of this part of the Isle of Dogs.

Pass most of London Yard and turn right to regain the River Walk up Amsterdam Road. See the slipway and expanse of stairs to a sand and gravelly shore where, in 1865, Alfred Yarrow established a large and famous shipbuilding firm. In 1906 it moved to the Scottish Clyde, where it continued to prosper.

Continue along the riverside past the tall Kelson House at Folly Wall, turn down River Barge Close to the left and then double back immediately, on the other side of a fence, up a narrow pathway to walk by the water once more in front of the pleasant riverside houses and gardens of **Capstan Square**.

31

Then, near to where there were once graving docks (dry docks), you will just catch a glimpse of it. Turn left and right. Then you just cannot miss this multi-coloured brick and garishly decorated building by the riverside, that when first seen I thought to be a giant playground toy, and on closer inspection imagined it to be a transplanted Egyptian jet engine factory. It is the apparently impregnable **ISLE OF DOGS PUMPING STATION**, where water is pumped away into the river on the rare occasions when the sewers might not be able to cope with rain from a storm. The "jet engines" at either end are for ventilation and decoration.

Having had a good look round this strange structure, return

to Manchester Road down a pathway in front of the Pumping Station and Galleon's View toward the **Queen of the Isle** pub. Turn right in Manchester Road and walk to nearby Manchester Road Bridge, more commonly known as the **Blue Bridge** (1969), an elegant, Dutch designed, single span (or lift) crossing over the main **dock entrance to the West India and Millwall Docks**.

Now, immediately after crossing the bridge, turn right into **Coldharbour**. In front of you is the 19th century **Gun** pub with its riverside terrace. To enjoy a pint here when the docks were in full swing was quite the best place on the river in which to relax and watch barges, tugs, coasters, banana boats, Baltic tramp steamers and ocean-going vessels negotiate the river tides and dock entrance. And when an old cargo ship left West India Dock in ballast, the partly exposed blades of the screw would crash into the water as she made headway. Only at very low tide was there little to see here. Now there is the Millennium site.

A short way along Coldharbour there is an 18th century house known as **Nelson House**. There are many stories about this house, the pub, Nelson, Lady Hamilton, trysts, goings-on and secret passages - most, if not all, to be taken with a good pinch of sea salt.

On the left hand side of Coldharbour once stood rather ramshackle warehouses for the storage of **Stockholm tar**. Naturally, the area around smelled gloriously (to me) of this liquid, used, I believe, for the preservation of coal sacks (another lovely smell) and the healing of foot rot in sheep. All gone, and now replaced by modern housing, I was walking past when trenches for foundations were being dug in 1997. What a treat it was to savour that very same smell of some 50 years ago. Over a long period of time the spillage of this tar must have permeated deep into the soil. Smells of Dockland continue to surface for our delight.

32

As you have to turn left at the end of Coldharbour, notice a pleasant bow-fronted house on your right at the river side of the old entrance to Blackwall Basin and Poplar Dock. This house, **Isle House**, built by **Sir John Rennie** in 1825 for the Dockmaster, will prepare you for a much finer house to appear shortly, built earlier by his father for a grander Dockmaster.

Turn right into busy Preston's Road, cross over the road and a bridge that has taken the place of a rattling, narrow, double-track swing bridge, and on the left you will see the magnificent **BRIDGE HOUSE**, in Bridge House Quay.

Built for the Principal Dockmaster between 1819 and 1820 to designs by **John Rennie Snr**. (the father of Sir John Rennie who built Isle House that we have just passed), this fine, bow-fronted (in both front and rear) house was strategically placed at the entrance to **Blackwall Basin** with uninterrupted views over both docks and River Thames. Its fluted Doric column porch feeds the first floor. Its equally spacious floor at ground level, seen from the now re-routed Preston's Road, was solely for staff and services. Even the Dockmaster found Bridge House to be too large and grand for him and was given an increase in salary to cope with the high cost of living there. Divided, then enlarged, used by the Fire Service, PLA Police, Customs, as flats, and now offices for the London Federation of Clubs for Young People, Bridge House has had a chequered career.

I remember it as a run down building some time in the 1950s to 1960s, with no-one able or willing to tackle the cost of restoration. It could so easily have been pulled down. Then a fire nearly destroyed it, consuming the roof in 1972. But there it stands today, restored, beautifully proportioned both in and out, and possibly the finest house in Docklands.

Continue, and just after Landons Close on the left, enter an archway leading to a spacious pathway beside **Poplar Dock** (1850), also known as Railway Dock. Here, colliers discharged their cargo directly into railway wagons on the quayside. It also once served as a reservoir for topping up the water level in West India Dock.

With Canary Wharf and Billingsgate Fish Market seen to your left over dock water, your route will sweep you down to a wide and desolate underpass beneath roads and rail and then up to **Blackwall** DLR Station. Here take a train back to Tower Gateway.

To take the DLR train from Blackwall Station in the other direction (Becton) will produce glimpses of the silo-like **Reuters** building by the now defunct **East India Dock** (the second enclosed dock after the Howland Great Wet Dock and originally called the **Brunswick Dock**), the **Financial Times** building, a multi-coloured **Tidal Pumping Station**, some old and none too interesting 1850 warehouses by **Royal Victoria Dock**, distant mills on the riverside, **London City Airport**, with the nice little **North Woolwich Old Station Museum** behind it, and a lot of complete bleakness where once the enormous **Royal Group of Docks** flourished.

If you have planned next to take Route 5, then return by DLR to Tower Gateway from Blackwall and board a District Line Underground train from Tower Hill (just a short walk from Tower Gateway) in the direction of Upminster. Then to follow Route 5, disembark at Bromley-by-Bow Station.

Or you may decide to take Route 6 on the south bank of the river from Tower Bridge. Tower Gateway (DLR) would still be your best destination. From there it is a short walk to the start at Tower Bridge (seen from the station exit).

ROUTE 5
JUST TO SEE THE TIDAL MILLS
(by foot roughly ¾ of a mile or 1.25 kilometres)

***This well worthwhile diversion (with instructions
above and below on how to get there by
Underground) is to see a piece of history that
is very much connected with the Thames,
dockland, barge traffic and London.***

33

Until the Industrial Revolution, corn was milled for flour in mills powered by wind or water. Wind force being unreliable and mill streams sometimes lacking water, tidal mills, especially to supply flour to London bakeries, used the guaranteed power of the tide as a source of energy.

As far up the river Thames as Teddington (Tide-end-town), tidal water, with two high tides every 24 hours, rose and fell in the river and up its many creeks and tributaries. This water passed through mill sluices and was trapped in creeks and ponds at high tide. Down went the tidal water toward the sea and that trapped behind the sluices was emptied back into the river beneath paddle wheels. These wheels were connected to mill stones which ground corn into flour.

Naturally, the tidal power was harnessed at every opportunity. Inlets, such as the Fleet, the Walbrook, the Neckinger (that flowed where St. Saviour's Dock is now), at Hermitage Basin, Wapping, Deptford Creek, Barking Creek and at many other tributaries, and especially up Bow Creek and the river Lea (or Lee), all had water mills to harness the power of tidal water. With the advent of steam power most disappeared. Their buildings were destroyed or used for other more lucrative purposes. One exception is the magnificent pair of tidal water mills at **Three Mill Lane** in Bromley-by-Bow (Three Mills because there was once another there).

Take the District Line Underground from Tower Hill, or any other convenient station, and disembark at **Bromley-by-Bow Station**. Turn left as you leave the station, take the underpass there beneath a very busy road, turn right as you leave it, carry on in the same direction, pass Tesco, and turn right, around the supermarket into Three Mill Lane. You will then come to two large **tidal mills**.

The older mill on the left is **THE HOUSE MILL**, built in 1776, the one in front of you, with two grain drying towers and a clock tower, is **THE CLOCK MILL** (1817). To the right is Bow Creek, and behind the mills to the left are the Bow Creek Back Rivers, a complex of waterways flowing through low land (once marsh) with names such as Three Mill Wall River, Waterworks River, City Mill River, Pudding Mill River and the River Lea. At one time there were at least nine water mills working in the district. Now only two survive for us to get a feel for the importance of tidal mills in their time. Under the guidance of the Lower Lea Project the whole area is in the course of regeneration. The detritus of modern civilisation is being dredged up and cleared away. Trees are being planted and river banks repaired and maintained.

The mills were not the only industries in the area. Others were gunpowder making, calico printing, tanning, porcelain manufacture, paper making and distilling.

From Holland, William III (of William and Mary), and returning soldiers, introduced the drink of gin to these islands, with deadly effect on its inhabitants in the 18th century. The mills turned from flour milling to the far more lucrative trade of distilling in the 1740s, and then back to flour milling with the feared food shortages during the Napoleonic wars.

Of timber construction (look at the back), House Mill is mostly faced with brick, secured to the main wooden structure by wall plates and rods. These prevented the brick wall from falling away under the intense vibration of milling. With its four 20' (6 metres) diameter undershoot water wheels it is the largest tidal mill existing in Great Britain (you can see some of the hefty machinery through the lower windows).

The Clock Mill, with three undershoot wheels, was built in 1817 to replace a previous mill. The clock tower, bell and clock face were retained from its 1750 predecessor. The two drying kilns are distinctive. In the days when grain was harvested at a slow pace, and thus subject to inclement weather, kilns such as these were essential to reduce the moisture content before milling could take place. Fire below heated the wheat on a floor above. Fumes and steam escaped from the cowls, the openings of which faced down wind under a weather vane principle, helping to create suction and prevent rain from entering the kiln.

Walk to the back of the House Mill and also through a narrow alleyway down the side of the Clock Mill to look at them from a different angle. Return to Bromley-by-Bow Station by taking the path through grass and by trees in front of the mills. Pass under two bridges. Cross **Bow Locks** by a concrete bridge for people and barge horses. Then look to the right where **Limehouse Cut** (mentioned on Route 2) joins the **River Lea**. Exit by a small gate and then a larger one, bearing right along Limehouse Cut. Take the underpass beneath the busy road, turn right at the end of it, and return up hill to the Underground.

To continue along Route 6, leave the train at Tower Hill Station and follow the directions below.

ROUTE 6

FROM TOWER BRIDGE TO ROTHERHITHE
(by foot roughly 1½ miles or 2.5 kilometres)

This route would once have taken you through a very busy part of inner docklands, known for its villainy, into a pleasant area of low lying countryside. Then the expansion of 19th century riverbank commerce smothered this countryside with a blanket of wharves, warehouses and domestic housing.

34

If you are continuing on Route 6, or if Route 6 is to be your first, and you are using the Underground system, reach Tower Hill Station on the District Line. Leave the station, take a kink to the left and then right to take an underpass. Turn left along a pathway, keeping the moat and the Tower of London on your right hand side. Take the underpass beneath Tower Bridge Road and climb the steps to the left. Cross St. Katharine's Way, which leads down to the river and St. Katharine Dock, and walk toward Tower Bridge on the downstream side.

The steel, granite and Portland stone confection of **TOWER BRIDGE** (opened in 1894 after eight years of construction and made to the design of John Wolfe Barry) is the very epitome of the Victorian's idea of size, decoration, craftsmanship and durability. Seen from both afar or close to, it represents a quite splendid example of the mark that those of the 19th century made on the architectural heritage of this country.

Its two counterweight bascules span 200' (70 metres) and can open in around one and a half minutes to allow tall ships into and out of the Upper Pool.

Stand on the pavement between the inner and outer arches of the bridge and look at the massive, riveted iron supports running between the main and outer towers. The designer's skill and constructor's craftsmanship in producing these laminated supports is marvellous to behold. They are true signs of a race that thought fearlessly and worked on a grand scale.

35

When you are standing on the left (downriver) side of the bridge, look to the south shore at a building right next to the bridge itself. It is the **ANCHOR BREWHOUSE**. The building consists of three parts, the Boilerhouse, the Brewhouse and the Malt Mill. I like the Boilerhouse, with its tall windows and integral chimney stack. Chimney stacks, once commonplace as a means of putting coal smoke high into the air, are now few and far between. Perhaps that is why they now look so imposing.

A brewhouse stood here before John Courage bought it in 1787. The buildings you are looking at date from around a hundred years later. There have been rebuildings and refurbishments since then.

Cross the bridge and take the steps down to the riverside on the left hand side as you leave it. Half way down you will come to one of those small and supremely simple items, created by an unknown genius, that appeal to me no end. It is a metal plate set into the corner of the stonework. You will see that there was another in the opposing corner, but that has now gone. What were or are they for? They stop men from urinating in the corner. Spent liquid simply flows back and soaks the trousers.

36

A t the bottom of these urine-free steps turn right to make off down **Shad Thames**, keeping the **Riverside Book Shop** on your right. After a short distance take a narrow alleyway (Maggie Blake's Cause) to your left past hidden rubbish bins and disinfectant smells. Now you will find yourself on the river bank with a fine view of **Tower Bridge** (ideal for photography). Keep to the bank, passing smart restaurants beneath **BUTLER'S WHARF** (originally 1873). This is a massive and imposing building best seen from the other side of the river or from its end. In its heyday the wharf handled tea and food of many kinds. Butler's, with Hay's Wharf on the other side of Tower Bridge, were often known as the "larder of London". Now Butler's Wharf is for restaurants, offices and living accommodation.

Beyond Butler's Wharf, and past a substantial anchor resting on the pathway, is the white, slab-sided **Design Museum**. To design a design museum must be a very difficult proposition, as whatever the outcome some are sure to criticise it as bad design. Here they have rightly opted for almost no design at all, except, perhaps as a throwback to German architecture of between the wars.

37

Now you will have to decide whether to carry straight on and cross **ST. SAVIOUR'S DOCK** (once Savory's

Dock) via a delicate stainless steel and wood bridge, or walk around St. Saviour's Dock via **Shad Thames** and **Mill Street**. I would recommend the walk around to savour a little of what it was like in the days before the docks were gentrified. So take the roadway beneath the Design Museum. Look at the warehouses and the roadway. Imagine the noise of cart wheels, the congestion and shouting that went with it, and the smell of teas and spices and the rattle of peas, rice and lentils that were handled there. Lorries and carts filled the street as goods were lowered by teams of warehousemen, crane operators and foremen. That was in daytime. At night-time there was almost total silence, and in a pea-soup fog - total silence. The scurrying rats were always quiet.

You will be able to look back down the dock when you reach the busy thoroughfare where Tooley Street becomes Jamaica Road. This was once the mouth of the river Neckinger, where there were tidal mills, but the flow was diverted and now gone. The name Neckinger may come from a Neckinger Wharf nearby, where Thames thieves were strung up by the "Devil's Neckcloth". Visualise the water or mud of the tidal dock, covered with barges, sometimes several deep, all tied to each other or moored to their warehouses. With the tide high, wash from ships or tugs would disturb the dock water. Then the barges would clang together. These, with the rattling of ground mooring chains and the noise of signals from tugs and ships telling others of their intended change of direction, were the river noises of dockland.

Many of the dockside warehouses are still there, cleaner it is true, but there still. No longer full of fragrant spices, they house offices and provide safe living accommodation in an area once known for its lawlessness. The warehouses are real dockland buildings, and here, at St. Saviour's Dock, is about the best and most evocative collection remaining.

38

Walk back through Mill Street on the downstream side of the dock warehouses and suddenly be amazed at the sight on the left hand side of a tall chimney stack with iron straps built in the form of a **CLASSICAL COLUMN** (there were two others like it on an early 19th century gas works near Regent's Park). This, part of an 1885 corn mill, was to extract the coal smoke from a steam boiler that powered the mill, grinding corn into flour. **New Concordia Wharf**, next to it, was a storage warehouse for grain, named after a mid western town in the USA from where much of it was imported. The warehouse has now been well converted into offices and flats. A pathway around the courtyard at the end of the road will lead you back to the stainless steel bridge across the river end of St. Saviour's Dock. So return to look down the dock from this direction if you missed it by taking the Shad Thames and Mill Street route.

39

At this corner, at the end of Mill Street, the road turns right to become Bermondsey Wall West. If you wanted to see fluting on the chimney stack column by New Concordia Wharf, you will now make up for it because, at this corner, the rear of **CHINA WHARF** (1988) is entirely fluted. Seen from the water, or the river side by the bridge over St. Saviour's Dock, you will see China Wharf to be one of the more imaginative buildings in Docklands. It sports fancy, modern ironwork balconies above the water, and a less modern but fun one below, taking the form of a boat's stern sticking out over the river above the high water mark.

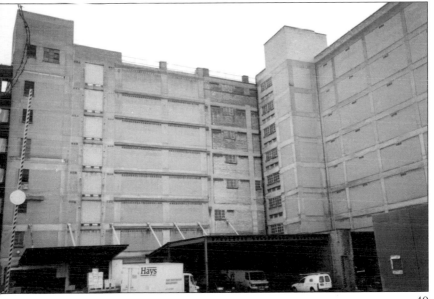

40

Walk down Bermondsey Wall West past the development of **Jacob's Island** (it really was once an island, and a pretty sordid one at that, so much so that Dickens had Sikes jumping to his death there in Oliver Twist) into Chamber's Street and stop to wonder at the enormous and almost featureless, concrete, once cold store warehouse of **CHAMBER'S WHARF**. Much of working docklands architecture was forbidding, featureless and as practical as this building. Sadly, some of the buildings that have replaced them are almost as featureless.

Turn left around Chamber's Wharf to the river again via Loftie Street. Enter Fountain Green Square. Keep to the river side and you will pass **Cherry Garden Pier** where since the 17th century the people of London would escape the ill odours of their cramped conditions, and then later, the soot and grime of Victorian industry, for pure air and cherry orchards. In busier times there was a headway board beside the pier, indicating the amount of headway for boats passing beneath the bascules of Tower Bridge upstream. There is a **primitive "Gents"** at the entrance to the pier, one that may have been there since Victorian days. Could Samuel Pepys perhaps have found its predecessor convenient in the 17th century when he landed here to buy cherries for his wife?

41

Continue by the riverside to look at 200 year old
CORBETT'S WHARF, at 87. Its fascinating iron
columns were cast for a specific task, with what appear to be
rails, with pulleys above, presumably for some form of
shuttering to close off the warehouse from the street. The

columns, one of which was cast with a flat surface to the rear, support timbers that, in turn, support four floors of warehouse brickwork above. Once owned by the warfingers Timothy Addis & Son, the warehouse was used for salt and spices. In the days when it was in use, I wonder if we would have taken notice of the fine, cast ironwork.

Soon you will reach a spot that is absolutely steeped in artistic and ancient history. Sunk in the folds of grass on your right are the remains of a **moated manor house**, thought to have been built for King Edward III (1327-1377). Not only was it in pleasant countryside, but was accessible by water - the easiest, probably safest, and most reliable form of transport at that time. It is possible that ships were made nearby, because in 1355 the King set sail for France from about this spot. He embarked with his army in 40 large vessels.

On the left is **THE ANGEL** pub of 15th century origins, though the present building is of Victorian construction. Although there are nowadays plenty of good places from which to view the river, in times when warehouses lined the banks there were but few. So the view from the Angel was then, and still is, one of the finest. Many artists, such as **Turner** and **Whistler**, and perhaps even Monet and Derain, have marvelled at the orange sun setting through the mist in the direction of the Tower of London, and the other way at the downstream water vista toward Limehouse, crowded with shipping at wharves, at anchor, or tied to buoys or tiers.

Many other famous people have enjoyed ale on the pub's wooden galleries hanging over the water. **Captain Christopher Jones** of the Mayflower was a frequenter, as was **Captain Cook**, **Samuel Pepys** and the infamous **Judge Jeffreys** (said to have come regularly to watch the hangings at Execution Dock across the river - though there were closer views, surely).

The pub is one of varied history and of a motley collection of clients. Having stood on the site since medieval times, it has been the haunt of sailors, dockers, watermen, brigands, vagabonds, cut-purses, gentry and artists. And I'm sure they will continue to visit the Angel.

43

More artistic heritage surfaces almost next door, for at the head of **FULFORD STREET** stands No.1. This building was once owned by Braithwaite and Dean, as were several others in this lost "terrace" of dateless, ramshackle houses/wharves. Also housing barge builders, barge owners, renters and repairers (G. Pace and William Moore among them), an enquiry agent called James Pink, warfingers and coffee rooms, they leaned precariously against each other and on stilts over the water. The terrace then stood alone, abandoned by its neighbours, except for the Angel. But what remained in the early post-war years attracted the artistic. **Edward Wolfe** the painter lived there, as did **Anthony Armstrong-Jones**, the photographer. Now only the one house survives, still twisted, but managing to stand fairly upright on its own.

It is about here, by the grassy mound of spoil on the right, that we leave Bermondsey for **Rotherhithe** (once known as **Redriffe**).

Before looking at more buildings, it is worth mentioning that you are about to enter a part of London that is absolutely steeped in maritime history. For it is around this bend of the river from Rotherhithe to Deptford and beyond, but mainly on the land lying between Rotherhithe Street and the river bank, that was, from medieval times until toward the end of the 1800s, the greatest ship building area of the country, and therefore the world. Its heyday was from between the mid 1600s to the mid 1800s, when both naval and merchant ships were constructed in quantity for war and trade. They were wooden sailing ships.

Rotherhithe shipbuilders were slow to embrace the age of steel and steam, one that was in full swing by the mid 19th century. Riverside property was then becoming of greater value as wharfage, warehousing and other trades. Supplies of suitable timber dwindled. There were strikes. Craftsmen's wages became higher than elsewhere. Ships became bigger, so space for building them in the constricted Rotherhithe yards became impossible. Then the Surrey Commercial Docks grew to become of greater importance than even the shipyards' final flourish of work in breaking up wooden ships to recover seasoned timber for house building and furniture making.

And of all this industry, that took place over such a long period of time, there is hardly a sign remaining. So your imagination will now be an important part of the pleasure to be gained from strolling along the Rotherhithe streets and riverside.

44

Continue along the riverside and pass **Prince's Tower**, a tall, white 1930s looking building, which, being so white, stands out along the river shore with the Design Museum as buildings that want to be noticed, rather than blending in with the rest. And they do stand out, especially when seen from the north bank.

Continue through a warehouse alleyway (Rotherhithe Street) until you come to **St. Mary's Church** in the heart of Rotherhithe. Just before you reach it, look through the churchyard to the right to see **ST. MARY, ROTHERHITHE, FREE SCHOOL**. Here, on the left of Rotherhithe Street, stands **Thames Tunnel Mills**, a well converted flour mill.

The Free School has, like St. John of Wapping School, sculpted and painted students, here on brackets, set on the venerable wall. The school was founded in 1613 and "removed here in 1797". With its 1821 **Watch House** (where the constable watched out for malefactors and grave robbers) it presents a past picture of a tight and bright sailing community, where presumably people knew each other and most had something to do with shipping in its many aspects. They must have been proud of this school. And sailors on the dangerous high seas would have taken comfort in the knowledge that their children were being well educated here.

This would not have been an area of good pickings for the Press Gang, most of the sailors in the district being volunteers, with the sea in their blood and blood lines. It would have been further afield that drunks and those not in church on Sunday would have been knocked on the head to find themselves aboard one of His Majesty's ships of war. One of my own ancestors was press ganged in Plymouth and jumped ship off Lincolnshire to swim ashore and settle in Liverpool.

St. Mary's Church has origins possibly in the Dark Ages. The present building was built in 1714, the tower being added in 1747. **Captain Christopher Jones**, Captain of the Mayflower, worshipped in an earlier church on the site and was buried in the churchyard in 1622. There are nautical elements in the church's construction. The steps up to it are flood prevention measures.

You now come to the mellow **Mayflower** pub close to the church. Once the Shippe and then the Spread Eagle, it is a 17th century hostelry with a small riverside platform on which to drink and view the water scenery.

Go down St. Marychurch Street if you want a closer look at St. Mary, Rotherhithe, Free School.

45

Continue along Rotherhithe Street and you will see on the right a plain brick building with a fun chimney at one end of it. This is **BRUNEL'S ENGINE HOUSE**, which used steam power to drain water from the under-river workings toward the end of his tunnel construction (1825-1843).

Sir Marc and Isambard Kingdom Brunel's tunnel, recently refurbished and used by the Underground Railway's East London Line, was **the world's first underwater tunnel of modern times** (the Babylonians and Romans having done it before). It was originally intended for horses, carts and carriages, but became only a foot tunnel until converted into one for full size steam trains in 1869. It crosses beneath the entrance ramp to the Rotherhithe Road Tunnel. And it is about where these two tunnels cross that you could take a train home if you are fatigued. To reach the station, continue, turn right into Railway Avenue and right into busy Brunel Road, where you will see the station immediately on the right. It is not far. On this East London Line are the stations: Whitechapel (for the District Line), Shadwell, Rotherhithe, Surrey Quays, New Cross and New Cross Gate.

From Tower Bridge you have now walked almost 1½ miles (2.5 km).

ROUTE 7

FROM ROTHERHITHE TO GREENWICH

(by foot roughly 3¾ miles or 6 kilometres, if taking the bus for part of it. But there is a "go home" point at Surrey Quays, near Greenland Dock 2 miles or 3.5 kilometres from Rotherhithe)

This route takes you along a riverside that was once the greatest ship building area in the world. Now hardly a vestige of it remains.

If starting off on Route 7, reach the beginning by taking the Underground East London Line to Rotherhithe Station. Turn left as you leave the station and then left again into Railway Avenue. Then turn right into Rotherhithe Street.

Otherwise, continue as before along Rotherhithe Street. Pass **Brandram's Wharf**, where an atrium has been formed within the warehouse, and **Charles Hay & Sons** (1789) barge building and repairers. Turn left into **Cumberland Wharf** to see typical Thames barges in the water. Keep to the river side. Pass some stairs and join Rotherhithe Street again. Then you will come to a bascule bridge that was raised to allow ships into an entrance to **Surrey Basin** and the **Surrey Commercial Docks**. The Basin was connected to 15 other docks and ponds, as well as a 3½ mile long canal.

These docks, starting with The Howland Great Wet Dock in about 1700, spread, after several amalgamations in the mid 19th century, to become the Surrey Commercial Docks, a huge area of warehousing, timber sheds, docks and ponds, almost covering the entire Rotherhithe bend of the river.

Always bleak, it was sometimes known locally as Dead Man's Dock, after a mass grave of plague victims was discovered. The dockers there, known as Deal Porters, were among the hardest working, humping enormous weights of timber on their shoulders.

Now the Surrey Commercial Docks have been mostly filled in and built over. But there were many, some deep (27'-31') to take ocean going ships and some, like Globe Pond, Lavender Pond, Acorn Pond, Centre Pond, Quebec Pond and Canada Pond were less deep and used for floating timber. These were the **timber ponds** that kept softwood moist, thus preventing it from splitting. When wanted up or downstream, "rafters" would tie together long lines of these logs and, headed by a man in a rowing boat, would use the flow of the tide to deliver their timber to its destination. These rafters would stand and walk around on the logs and never fall into the water.

By the bascule bridge note the **Spice Island** pub on the left, well positioned on the river bank for Thames vistas.

Now the walking can get as monotonous as the architecture. So regain the Thames Path up steps at King and Queen Wharf. Keep to the river bank whenever possible for views across the water. It is a good time to imagine the hustle and bustle of 18th century shipbuilding along this whole stretch.

Whether you are walking on the river side or in Rotherhithe Street, you will reach the entrance to **Lavender Pond**. The enormous Lavender Dock and Acorn Timber Pond were once connected to the river by a lock. Now, part of Lavender Dock has become a charming little nature reserve. Cross the road to see it. The red brick Pumphouse (1930, and now a little museum) between the dock and the river, topped up water levels in the Surrey Commercial Docks. The first ship to be built at the waterside here was in 1757.

Return to the riverside, and when you reach Pageant Stairs and Wharf, and the **obelisk**, you are pretty well at **Cuckold's Point**. Also marked on maps as Cuckholds and Cucknold's, it is so named, rather fancifully, after an incident in the early 13th century when King John was found in a compromising position with the wife of a local flour miller. As compensation, the King was obliged to give the offended miller a stretch of the foreshore. Another theory is that it was named after the site of a ducking stool, with cattle horns marking the spot.

But whatever the reason, it is from just beyond here that you can look across the river up **Limekiln Creek** to a two studio house that the present owners believe was the first warehouse in Docklands to be converted into living accommodation (1964-5). That I did it is by the bye.

Right by where you are now standing, with a view up Limekiln Creek, there was, when I lived across the water, a large lead mill run by H.J. Enthoven Ltd. It had two tall chimneys, known locally as "melting chimneys".

This is a good place from which to view **Canary Wharf** across the river.

Soon, where there are wooden stairs to the river, you will come to **Canada Wharf**, another warehouse nicely converted to living accommodation.

46

Now, at last, you come to a fine house on the left in an old shipbuilding and repair yard known as **Nelson Dock**. It is **NELSON HOUSE**. Its name had nothing to do with Lord

Nelson. With octagonal cupola and river look-out, this house was built for one of the wealthy owners of Nelson Dock in 1740. It is really pleasant to come across such a lovely building after so many uninspiring creations along the river, just as it is so exciting to find the vestiges of a real dockyard in a district that was once almost all dockyards. So this is a treasured spot, even though the site is shared by an hotel.

A shipbuilding and repair yard has been on this site since ships were first built on the Rotherhithe bank of the river - the earliest records discovered being from 1687. Nelson Dock was so named, in all probability, after one of its owners. The name is comparatively new, as for most of its working life the dock was called Cuckold's Point, even though Cuckold's Point is a little way upriver.

The dock was always one of the busiest and largest on this Rotherhithe bank, its several slipways and dry docks being in constant use under many owners, spanning from the late 17th century to the advent of steam and then screw-driven ships in the late 19th century. It even continued as a repair dock until the 1960s, in the hands of Mills & Knight.

What remains to be seen is an **engine house and draw dock**, in which stands La Dame de Serk, a French three masted barque, built in 1952, and a **water-filled dry dock**, now a decoration. The head of this disused dry dock is retained on the roadside by old **ships' plates.**

These items of a working dock remain at Nelson Dock. They are there and they are real - real reminders of a bygone age of maritime endeavour, sweat and, sadly, in the case of many of the docks, periodic bankruptcy (usually at the conclusion of wars or national frights, when new ships were no longer required for the Navy).

Now comes a dull stretch and then a bit of jiggery-pokery walking around buildings. Continue past a Jubilee Line ventilation shaft and at **Surrey Dock Farm** (ideal for children), turn right and skirt around the farm with its bucolic smells, turning left into Vaughn Street to regain the Thames Path at

Barnard's Wharf (another renowned shipbuilding yard operating from the mid 18th to mid 19th centuries). Turn right by a red crane into Commercial Pier Wharf and first left, still in Commercial Pier Wharf. Pass New Caledonian Wharf, in what has become Odessa Street, and turn left up Randall Rents (where shipyard workers once lived) to the river once more. That last bit of river walk may be opened up. Continue by the river and you come to **Greenland Dock** on the right.

Enter the dock and walk down the right hand side along Finland Quay East, keeping the dock water and ships on your left. Find a seat. Look at the dock. Peer into history.

In 1696 the Howland family promoted a Bill of Parliament to construct an inland dock (the first) to protect merchantmen from the vagaries of tidal water, ice and storm. It was also for fitting out, to work in conjunction with the Royal Dockyard nearby ("...convenient of the Dock for His Majesty's ships"), and to allow cooks to prepare meals ashore, thus preventing fire from burning the wooden vessels to the water line. With the main dock completed around 1700, docks and slipways were also constructed at the riverside for building, fitting out and repair of ships - mostly East Indiamen. It was a pleasant place with smells of the countryside, of sawn timber and boiling tar.

Although there was much theft on the river at that time, a walled dock for the protection of ships and goods had not yet been considered. The only wind break for the full complement of 120 large vessels were several rows of deciduous trees. And it worked. In a violent storm in 1703, most of the ships on the river dragged their moorings and foundered on the north shore. Only one ship in the **Howland Great Wet Dock** suffered damage.

You are looking at that very dock - though since enlarged. It was later to be named the Greenland Dock and used for the fish, whale oil and blubber trades - when an unpleasant smell joined those of nature. Eventually it was connected to other docks to form the Surrey Commercial Docks for the timber, grain, foodstuff and wine trades.

47

Having absorbed how important this tract of dock water has been in the past, rise and continue along the dock side to the **Norway Cut** double swing bridge. Turn right and cross Finland Street to **PLOVER WAY**. In part of the one-time Norway Dock, the houses before you have been built at the edge or, each with its own wooden bridge, over the water on stilts. With plants, and duck-resting rafts in the pond, these mini castles with a moat form a most attractive Dockland housing complex. Walk around the pond if you feel like it.

From Plover Way walk back to Greenland Dock. At the top of the dock (to the right), and through a tunnel under a huge bascule bridge, is **Surrey Quays Shopping Centre** (P14 bus to Limehouse DLR), and beyond it, **Surrey Quays Underground**, on the East London Line. So here, after 2 miles or almost 3.5 kilometres from Rotherhithe, is a get-out point if you want to go home. Or you could skip the rest of

Route 7 and go from here to Greenwich by bus. If so, take a 188 either from outside Surrey Quays Shopping Centre or on Lower Road, by Surrey Quays Underground Station. Alight, en route, at Deptford High Street to see the interesting terrace of early 18th century houses.

48

Go back to the river side, turn right, and walk through to the next dock in line to the south. This is **Greenland South Dock**, with its lock, pleasure craft and, at the far end, the tall building of **BALTIC QUAY** (1990).

There is something grand about Baltic Quay's arched roof tower and other four arches. Grand, that is, when seen from a distance. The top of the construction appears to be surrounded by scaffolding. Nearer to, this turns out to be support for balconies. The building becomes less "human" as you approach it - colder and more impersonal. But it is very much a Dockland building with its upturned hull shapes, and a brave one at that.

Continue along the River Walk. Across the water you will see the old entrance to Millwall Outer Dock. Pass an old **boundary stone** at the end of a short and isolated wall, telling that you are leaving Surrey for Kent.

You will soon see the tall building, **Aragon Tower**, with the earlier-mentioned moulded face masks (Route 1, page 27), giving a plain building some interest at ground level.

49

Soon after Aragon Tower you will come to the 1780s rum warehouses of the **ROYAL VICTORIA VICTUALLING YARDS** ("Victoria" only after Queen Victoria's visit in 1858). These were part of a huge complex of buildings that supplied the Navy at home and overseas with everything they wanted, from rum and pickled meat to hard tack and needles. The yards opened in 1742 and closed in 1961.

Around here, in 1581, possibly by the gate to the river or foreshore, or up a no-longer existing creek nearby, or even at Greenwich, **Queen Elizabeth I** knighted **Francis Drake** on the Golden Hind for his "Circuiting 'round about the whole earth" in the years 1577-1581.

Beyond the Victualling Yards, Royal ships were being repaired in 1420. In 1513 Henry VIII established "a great storehouse" and "a Royal Station for ships" here, which grew into being the **Royal Naval Dockyard**, or King's Yard. This stretched as far as Prince Street, off Evelyn Street. In 1665 Pepys records that he crossed from here in Deptford to the Isle of Dogs. He must have been inspecting ships on the slipways or in the dockyard. The Royal Naval Dockyard closed in 1869. The land was then used as the Foreign Cattle Market (1871-1913), and after that a wharf for importing newsprint from Scandinavia.

You can no longer walk by the river, so return to Aragon Tower and turn left down the near side of it to pass a fine **terrace of 18th century Officers' Houses**. Then, at the end of this terrace, branch off to the right to exit from the **Main Gate** of the Victualling Yards, passing **colonnaded Naval Officers' Quarters** and Porter's Lodge. The Gate is adorned with fouled anchors and animal skulls. The size of the cannon bollards outside it is impressive.

As you exit into Grove Street turn right and catch a 199 bus just up on the right hand side. It passes every 10-15 minutes. Ask the driver or passengers to tell you where to alight for **Deptford High Street**. As the stop is beyond the High Street, you will have to walk back and turn left to reach it.

50

When in Deptford High Street, walk up it, past Manze's Eel and Pie Shop at 204 on the left, and then turn left into **ALBURY STREET** (originally Union Street).

On the left you will soon see a really fine **Queen Anne terrace** of houses built by a bricklayer as a speculative venture between 1706 and 1717. Known as **The Captains' Houses**, they were constructed for senior naval officers. The carved door surrounds that remain after theft and vandalism are outstanding, sometimes looking almost too grand for the houses. But the street is a jewel among dross, and thus comes as a complete and stunning surprise. At the far end the houses are to be seen on both sides of the cobbled street, giving an even better idea of what it must have been like there almost 300 years ago. How very lucky it is for us that they survive - in whatever state.

There is not a great deal of interest to see in Deptford High

Street. But a short detour up past its multiracial shops to the market beyond the railway bridge will reveal a most pleasant yellow stock, red brick and acanthus-terracotta-patterned building on the left, and on the right, an 1895 building (both above shop fronts). Then, at the end on the right, comes a fine bow-fronted **Regency house**. You may also have seen **St. Paul's Church** (designed by Thomas Archer in 1730 and some thinking it to be the finest baroque church in England) on the left. And down Frankham Street, also on the left, there is the decorated building mentioned in Route 1 (page 27).

Return to take a 188 or 199 bus to Greenwich from the stop where you alighted.

On the left as you set out by bus were once the extensive boatyards of the East India Company (from 1601 until the late 1700s). On site they made almost all that was wanted in the way of shipping and items for their support. Here the timber was sawn in saw pits and ships were constructed on building slips at the riverside. They made the masts, yards, rope and sails, anchors and anchor chains. Cattle were slaughtered and the meat salted down. Gunpowder and shot were manufactured.

You will pass over **Deptford** (Depe Ford) **Creek**, once a hive of shipping activity and where the first bridge was constructed in 1004. The **Ravensbourne River** and its tidal water once powered many water mills. These mills are mentioned in the **Doomsday Book** (1086), when five thousand water mills were counted in England.

Route 7 ends at the 188 bus stop outside the Royal Naval College, Greenwich. From here Route 8 starts, once more by foot. Bus 199 stops in Nelson Road nearby, and you will need to retrace your steps a little and then turn right into King William Walk to continue on Route 8.

ROUTE 8

GREENWICH AND THE THAMES TO THE EAST

(by foot roughly 1¾ miles or 3 kilometres, not counting a continuation to the Millennium site or the Thames Barrier)

This route takes you past some lovely houses to a fine view over London from Greenwich Park. Then there is a short riverside stroll by three excellent pubs with river views.

51

If selecting Route 8 as your first, reach Island Gardens on the DLR, pass through the Greenwich Foot Tunnel, and walk past the starboard side (left as you look at the bow) of the Cutty Sark to reach the bus stops in King William Walk.

For Route 8, continue along **King William Walk** and away from the river and the **Cutty Sark** clipper ship (we come back to that later). Cross the busy Nelson Road/Romney Road intersection. Walk on (past **public conveniences** on the left, where dogs are not allowed) toward **Greenwich Park**, and at St. Mary's Gate turn right into Nevada Street. Now turn left uphill beside the park into **Croom's Hill**.

Pass or visit the **Fan Museum** and admire the fine **17th, 18th and 19th CENTURY PARK SIDE HOUSES** and take any right hand turn and back for further pleasant viewing (especially Gloucester Circus) until you are able to enter **Greenwich Park** on the left at King George Street Gate, near a grand **18th century terrace**. There was a Roman settlement in the park from 49-350 AD.

52

Walk as straight as you can across the hill in front of you, crossing a road as you do so, and climb a path that curves up to the right toward the **OLD ROYAL**

OBSERVATORY AND TIMEBALL. The Old Royal Observatory in Greenwich Park was the first purpose-built scientific building in England. It was commissioned by Charles II, designed by Sir Christopher Wren in 1675, and paid for by selling off some barrels of old gunpowder.

From the **Observatory**, where Longitude Zero and Greenwich Mean Time (GMT) are measured, the red **Timeball** has fallen down its mast at exactly 1300 hours (at mid-day the astronomers were too busy measuring the sun) since it was erected in 1833. To this day, it has enabled navigators, within telescope distance on the Thames, to set their chronometers with absolute accuracy. A dockland building like this (with a ball mobile combined) makes it very special indeed.

Look down at a glorious landscape, over the **Queen's House** (designed by Inigo Jones in 1616, and built for James I), the **National Maritime Museum** and Wren's **Royal Naval College** (more on this shortly), toward the river, Isle of Dogs, Canary Wharf and central London.

Return to where you first saw the park at St. Mary's Gate and Nevada Street, and retrace your steps down King William Walk, past the bus stops and the side of the Royal Naval College, to see the **Cutty Sark** clipper ship in its permanent dry dock. She was named after a poem by Robert Burns called Tam O'Shanter, where a pretty girl wore only a "cutty sark" (a short shirt of Paisley linen). Built in Scotland and launched in 1869, she plied her trade on the seven seas with cargoes mainly of tea and wool.

Beyond the Cutty Sark is the **Greenwich Pier**, where you might now, or later, return to the Tower of London, Charing Cross or Westminster by boat (your One Day Travelcard will not cover the cost of this journey). Turn right down a pathway by the pier entrance to walk beside the river in front of the **ROYAL NAVAL COLLEGE** (which moved here from Portsmouth in 1873).

These Sir Christopher Wren buildings were built toward the end of the 17th century on the site of the Tudor Palace of Placentia. The spoil was used to form the riverside walk. Designed as a Palace also, it became a hospital for disabled seamen. Impressive for the power and weight of design, these buildings are best seen at a distance from Island Gardens across the river on the Isle of Dogs, or from high up in Greenwich Park near to the Old Royal Observatory and Timeball. The design then becomes less weighty. The two domes gave Wren some practice before tackling the design of the much larger dome of St. Paul's Cathedral in the City.

From the river bank's wrought iron gateway you will get a good view of the College's spacious lawns, a framed view of Inigo Jones's **Queen's House** and the **Old Royal Observatory** and **Timeball** on the hill beyond.

54

Continue along the riverbank to the Regency style **TRAFALGAR TAVERN** (1815). This is a fine bow-fronted building overlooking the Thames. Whitebait feasts were a feature here in earlier times. The pub still serves this delicacy.

55

Walk along the alleyway (Crane Street) behind the Trafalgar, past the **Yacht** pub (another with a good view of the river) to **TRINITY HOSPITAL**, an almshouse founded by the Earl of Northampton in 1613. It was built (not with the Victorian decorations to the front) from between 1613 and 1617 for retired gentlemen who had lived in Greenwich for at least four years, and eight pensioners traditionally coming from Norfolk. In summer you might catch a glimpse of its pleasant gardens through the open doorway.

Continue as close to the river as possible under where cranes grabbed coal from the holds of colliers (known as Flat Irons). These ships plied their trade between here and Newcastle or Swansea bringing coal for the power station (1906) that provided electricity for London's trams. Then swirling coal dust got into the eyes and grime was thick under foot.

56

Now, almost right away, you will reach the **CUTTY SARK** pub at 4-6 Ballast Quay, the last building I have chosen on Route 8.

The ale house faces the river, with Georgian bow-fronts boldly displaying its name. The pub building you see is late Georgian, but its origins are 17th century.

Its grand upstairs room overlooks the river. If the weather is fine, there are benches and tables on the riverbank where you may also eat and drink.

On the right hand side of the river bend in front of you, beyond where you may see boats discharging sand and gravel, stood the Submarine Cable Works. Graceful, white, cable-laying ships moored here to take on cable for the beds of oceans around the world. The first Atlantic cable, laid by the Great Eastern, was made here.

Possibly continue on foot to the **Millennium site**, which you will see downstream across the bend of the river, or even to the **Thames Barrier** (another 2¾ miles or 4.5 kilometres). Return to Greenwich for a waterborne trip back to central London. Or possibly walk through the Greenwich foot tunnel (the pipe), taking the lift in the rotunda near to the clipper ship, and then the Docklands Light Rail from Island Gardens back to Bank or Tower Gateway stations via Canary Wharf.

In this book I have tried to point out buildings or parts of them that have interested me, and then set my ideas into words of dockland and historical interest. It would delight me if you have shared my pleasures.

INDEX

ABOUT THE AUTHOR

After a broken education in England and America, Jim Page-Roberts joined the RAF to become a pilot shortly before the end of WW2. Invalided out with TB, the disease returned when he was a medical student.

After art and theatre design schools he designed and painted scenery for the theatre and television.

Returning to fine art, he exhibited paintings in London and abroad. About to show large sculptures in elm wood, a car accident forced him to change course.

He then wrote many articles for magazines and newspapers, mainly on the subjects of wine and gardening.

His first book, in 1982, was on vines. This was followed by four on wine, a cookbook, and one on vines and wines.

He established The Mudlark Press in 1997. This is his third book under that imprint.

BIBLIOGRAPHY

History of the Port of London (volumes 1&2),
Sir J.G. Broodbank, Daniel O'Connor, 1921.

Port of London,
D.J. Owen, Port of London Authority, 1927.

Peepshow of the Port of London,
A.G. Linney, Sampson Low, Marston & Co., 1930.

Limehouse Through Five Centuries,
J.G. Birch, The Sheldon Press, 1930.

London's Lost Riverscape,
edited by Chris Ellmers and Alex Werner, Viking, 1988.

Ben's Limehouse,
B. Thomas, Ragged School Books, 1987.

On the River,
Pam Schweitzer and Charles Wegner, Age Exchange, 1989.

Shipbuilding in Rotherhithe - An Historical Introduction,
Stuart Rankin, Dockside Studio, 1997.

Shipbuilding in Rotherhithe - The Nelson Dockyard,
Stuart Rankin, Dockside Studio, 1996.

Shipbuilding in Rotherhithe - Greenland Dock & Barnard's
Wharf,
Stuart Rankin, Dockside Studio, 1997.

Docklands,
Stephanie Williams, Phaidon Press Limited, 1996.

London Under London,
Richard Trench and Ellis Hillman, John Murray, 1996.

The East End Nobody Knows,
Andrew Davies, Macmillan, 1990.

London's East End,
Jane Cox, Weidenfeld and Nicolson, 1994.

Available from
The Mudlark Press,
PO Box 13729, London W6 9GN.

DOCKLAND BUILDINGS OLD AND NEW,

£5.95 (+£1 for postage and packing).
"... a splendid piece of work"
- Andrew Davies. International lecturer and guide.

GUIDE TO A DOCKLAND OF CHANGE,

£4.95 (+£1 for postage and packing).
"Every step crammed with history, of anecdote, of smells and sights of a dockland past"
- East London Advertiser.

CANARY WHARF AND SIGHTS FROM DOCKLANDS LIGHT RAIL,

£2.95 (+50P for postage and packing).
"A must for those travelling down to Docklands"
- Port of London.

Notes on other dockland buildings and items of interest